The 401(k) Game-Changer

Structuring a Winning Retirement Plan

Carl Valimont

The 401(k) Game-Changer

Copyright © 2016, Carl Valimont

Published in the United States of America

ISBN-13: 978-1520839752

Here's What's Inside...

Without the help of others this book would not have become a reality. My sincere appreciation and gratitude goes out to the team:

Theresa Deuel
Angel Hessel
Tom Keating
Dan Ringsred
Jeff Rochon
Nancy Valimont

Introduction

In a Fog

Imagine you are on an early-morning walk on a foggy day in the city. You hear the distant sounds of a frantic, fever-pitched game. Curious, you make your way closer and realize it's the Winter Classic hockey game.

You take a seat to catch the action. The game is exciting, as both teams race up and down the ice. Because you can't see the scoreboard from your vantage point due to the fog, you feel a little left out.

After 15 minutes, the buzzer sounds. As the teams meet at center ice to shake hands, the weather clears enough for you to see the final score.

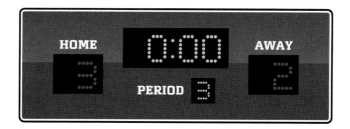

After decades of experience in sports and business (both playing and coaching hockey), I've come to realize a few universal truths. First and foremost, we need to know where we are—

1

or have a map that we can figure out or a chauffeur who has been there before.

It doesn't matter who you are, where you are, or how sure you are, there is always room to improve. A coach's primary mission is to figure out how to improve the team's results. Often the really successful coaches have specific processes that are repeatable and that act as maps for the players to buy into.

The purpose of this book is to share valuable strategies regarding the process I've developed and refined throughout the years to serve your 401(k) plan. Amazingly, the similarities between coaching a sport and advising 401(k) plan sponsors to win more often are striking. The results that flow from implementing a successful process are powerful. Sometimes it's about the scoreboard, but most of the time, it's about where the puck is and who has it.

The Strategic Game Plan – Our 5-Step Process

There can be many reasons why companies do not have the retirement plan process they want to have. Whether it is due to a lack of expertise or time, it exposes the employer and all of the employees to lost opportunities. Even though the possibility of litigation may be a distant concern, it still may cross your mind.

An optimal plan utilizes a proven process. I have found that the following steps are critical to helping your 401(k) achieve peak performance:

1. Identify current challenges and exposures.

2. Develop a winning strategy.

3. Properly position members of the team.

4. Execute the game plan consistently.

5. Monitor results and document.

We manage the entire due diligence process as part of our extensive service model, so plan sponsors can focus on the day-to-day priorities of their enterprises.

Chapter 1: Preparing for Success

Passion of the Game

After many years of playing professional hockey, I knew it was time to move on. Because I was still passionate about the game and its camaraderie, coaching was a natural transition for me. It allowed me to remain in an environment I love.

I learned that transitioning from athlete to coach required a different mindset. Success as an athlete does not automatically translate to coaching. I knew the rules of the game and how the positions were to be played. However, as a coach, I had to learn how to inspire, teach, help, and communicate effectively with others.

An important responsibility of a coach is to learn how to prepare athletes for peak performance. Training athletes has become a holistic activity that focuses on the entire athlete. Since the beginning of sport competition, athletes have sought to acquire the skills and knowledge of sports in order to become champions. Over the past 30 years, educational training programs have evolved in an effort to assist coaches and athletes to develop methods and strategies for achieving peak performance. In designing a coaching or educational program, you must ask, "How do we get from where we are to where we want to go?"

The Issues Plaguing 401(k) Retirement Plans

The strategies that coaches use can also apply to plan sponsors and/or committee members who are responsible for their companies' 401(k) plans. There are many issues to consider. Understanding how their employees think about saving for retirement, the exposures that the plan fiduciary face, the plan design choices that are available and improved employee appreciation are essential for an optimal 401(k) plan.

When people talk about America's retirement crisis, they typically comment on the failure of employees to save enough for retirement, but shortcomings in the 401(k) process itself are a looming issue for many plan sponsors. America has become a society plagued by borrowing and an "I-have-to-have-it-now" mentality. It's no secret that many of us simply don't save enough. **In 2015 the average U.S. household carried $15,762 in credit card debt and $130,922 in total debt.**

The huge burden of previous personal debt is keeping the average savings rate in America somewhere **between 3% to 4%.** As a result, the average account balance in a company-sponsored 401(k) plan is between **$45,000 and $75,000**. It is clear that a majority of Americans will not have enough retirement savings to continue their lifestyles later on. This will force them to go into overtime or rely on the government for financial assistance. Those "players" need "coaching" to develop a more effective game plan for their own retirements.

We want to help your employees to better understand and appreciate how valuable your "golden goose" retirement plan is for the golden eggs they want and need for their golden years.

Time and money have at least one characteristic in common: You either tell them where to go, or you wonder where they went! Habits only come in two flavors: effective and ineffective. At times, coaching is needed to help others get on the track they aspire to in order to achieve their peak performance.

Some employees may assume that they can't currently afford to participate in their retirement plans. The unmistakable reality is that they can't afford not to. This is the only opportunity they have to send more to their futures than the amount of reduction to their take-home pay due to the leverage of the tax break.

According to a recent study by Empower Institute of *4,000* American workers between the ages of *18 and 65*, the median individual is only on track to replace *62%* of his or her working income in retirement. The study provides a comprehensive overview of Americans' current readiness for retirement.

Lifetime Income Score (LIS)

MEDIAN LIS (2015)	MEDIAN LIS (2016)
58%	62%

The Lifetime Income Score^SM (LIS) report includes survey results from more than 4,000 American workers age 18 to 65. Based on individual responses, it estimates the percentage of working income — the LIS — that American households are on track to replace in retirement.

The LIS metric includes projected Social Security benefits (if available), defined benefit and defined contribution assets, personal savings, home equity and business ownership.

Distributed by GWFS Equities, Inc.

Who Is a Fiduciary?

A fiduciary is a person or an entity named in the written plan document or through a process described in the plan as having control over the plan's operation. A plan must have at least one fiduciary named in the written plan document. This person/entity will use discretion in administering and managing a plan or controlling the plan's assets. Many of the actions involved in operating a plan can cause the person or entity performing them to be a fiduciary. Fiduciary status is based on duties performed and not just a person's title.

The Significance of Being a Fiduciary

While playing hockey for the Milwaukee Admirals in the late 1980s, each player decided how to approach the off-season. Certain players trained alone, while others hired personal trainers. Almost without fail, the players who hired personal trainers, who used proven training techniques, pushed them out of their comfort zone, and held them accountable were in better shape for the season.

Being well prepared mitigates risk and increases one's chance of a successful outcome. It isn't an accident that so many professional athletes have personal trainers and nutritionists today.

Fiduciaries have important responsibilities and are subject to standards of conduct because they act on behalf of participants in retirement plans and their beneficiaries.

These responsibilities include:

- Acting solely in the interest of plan participants
- Following the plan documents
- Diversifying plan investments
- Paying only reasonable plan expenses
- Prudency when carrying out their duties
    - Focus on the process for making fiduciary decisions

This requires expertise in a variety of areas, such as investing. When lacking that expertise, a fiduciary will want to hire someone with professional knowledge to carry out investment duties as well as other functions. When hiring any plan service provider, a fiduciary may want to interview a number of potential providers, asking for the same information and providing the same requirements. By doing so, a fiduciary can document the process and make a meaningful comparison and decision.

Chapter 2: Identifying Challenges and Exposures

What Are Your Current Exposures?

As a fiduciary, it is important for the plan sponsor to manage risk by implementing and following a process. The process should involve an ongoing evaluation of each investment option in accordance with your Investment Policy Statement, which clearly states the performance standards and the methodology for replacing underperforming funds.

With growing litigation in this area, it is a good practice to have a clearly defined process behind choosing funds and being able to demonstrate the basis behind those decisions.

See 401(k) help center link for companies that have been sued, such as Boeing, Anthem®, Cigna®, and Caterpillar®: www.401khelpcenter.com

We have designed the following list of questions to assist you in fulfilling your fiduciary responsibilities. **Please take a moment to answer the questions on the next page:**

10 Key Questions

QUESTION	
1. As a 401(k) plan sponsor are you concerned about aspects of your fiduciary responsibilities, and question if you are doing enough to minimize your liability?	YES NO
2. Are you worried that a given service provider may have hidden conflicts of interest?	YES NO
3. Are you unsure if the investment options in the plan are adequate?	YES NO
4. Are you uncertain if the fees being paid are reasonable?	YES NO
5. Do you currently have an Investment Policy Statement?	YES NO
6. Does the current Investment Policy Statement outline a fund evaluation process? If so, under what circumstances would a fund be removed or replaced?	YES NO
7. Do you currently have an internal fund evaluation process in place for reviewing your investment lineup quarterly?	YES NO
8. Do you receive a quarterly fund perfomance review from the current provider? If so, who is responsible for reviewing the report to identify underperforming funds?	YES NO
9. Do you currently have a fund designated as your Qualified Default Investment Alternative (QDIA)?	YES NO
10. Does your current broker or advisor… a. Acknowledge in writing that they are a plan fiduciary? b. Provide a prudent fiduciary process for monitoring investment options? c. Provide you with investment advice and put it in writing?	YES NO

We see many companies managing their plans both correctly and incorrectly. One example of a company doing it incorrectly was a plan sponsor who told us that they had a 25-year relationship with a broker/dealer and that he had everything covered regarding their 401(k). After they agreed to allow us to review their document to provide a wellness check, we informed them that their plan didn't have a process in place for monitoring the investment lineup. Once they understood the importance of having a proven process, they also learned that they had over 10 severely underperforming funds in their lineup. Not surprisingly, they decided to change advisors despite the long-term relationship.

Being responsible for your plan means considering many things. Having a process for all responsibilities is an important step for those who manage plans.

The Challenges of "Doing It Myself"

There are basically two types of retirement plan participant investors. The first type knows—or thinks they know—how to invest their money. They are self-motivated and have a real interest in managing their own investment choices. The second type doesn't know and/or doesn't want to know how to invest their money or what investment options they should choose. They don't have the time, the patience, or the education to make informed investment decisions on an ongoing basis.

Studies indicate that **85%** of employees are in the don't know/don't want to know category.

401(k) Plan Participants

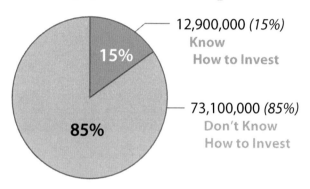

12,900,000 *(15%)*
Know
How to Invest

73,100,000 *(85%)*
Don't Know
How to Invest

The 401(k) may have become America's largest casino. There are 86 million 401(k) participants as I write this book. Many plans have 30 or more investment options. While many employees and plan sponsors may feel that a multitude of choices is an advantage, it may not be the case. An abundant number of choices can be confusing to the average employee—that 85%. Left to their own devices, they either choose not to invest because they're confused, or, worse, they make incorrect investment decisions based on being uninformed about investment information.

The average investor *(85% of the working population)* is likely to make investment choices like they are betting on sports teams. They expect both winning teams and losing teams to react in the future as they did in the past. If 85% of employees are in the, don't know/don't want to now category, then doesn't it make sense to help them with the investment decision process? When their 401(k) account is growing, a good employee becomes a better employee.

Keeping Emotions in the Holster

Emotions are a huge part of professional hockey. In the heat of battle, a player can let them get out of control. While playing for the Milwaukee Admirals, a teammate of mine got into a fight during the game with a player from the opposing team. They both received a penalty and were sent to the penalty box.

Our player was so irate and could not control his anger to the point that he scaled the partition separating the penalty boxes during the penalty and fell over the glass to get to the player on the other side. He was assessed a misconduct penalty and ejected from the game.

That additional penalty was a game-changer, as the opponent scored while we played short-handed. Ultimately, out-of-control and irrational emotions cost us the game!

Our emotions can energize us to overcome seemingly impossible challenges, or they can cause us to collapse under the pressure. Emotions can be an asset or a liability, but one thing is certain: They arrive without warning. It is common knowledge among professional investment advisors that emotional reactions while investing rarely create peak performance.

Let's analyze a few emotions that, when left unchecked, will greatly undermine long-term investment success.

The Confusion of Investing "On My Own"

Justin Kruger and David Dunning from the Department of Psychology at Cornell University published a study called "Unskilled and Unaware of It: How Difficulties in Recognizing One's Own Incompetence Lead to Inflated Self-Assessment" in the December 1999 issue of the *Journal of Personality and Social Psychology*.
It demonstrated over and over that when people are asked to rate their level of expertise in a variety of areas, the majority put themselves in the 'above average' category. However, after they are tested, the results repeatedly showed that a large percentage grossly overestimate their ability.

Abstract: People tend to hold overly favorable views of their abilities in many social and intellectual domains. The authors suggest that this overestimation occurs, in part, because people who are unskilled in these domains suffer a dual burden: Not only do they reach erroneous conclusions and make unfortunate choices, but their incompetence robs them of the metacognitive ability to realize it. Across four studies the authors found that participants scoring in the bottom quartile on tests grossly overestimated their test performances and abilities. ***Although their test scores put them in the 12th percentile, they estimated themselves to be in the 62nd.*** [1]

They accurately named this group the "unskilled and unaware." Unfortunately, this overconfidence makes people believe that any success they achieve is due solely to their decisions. That's a mistaken belief for many, and it is hard to change.

Irrational Exuberance

Studies have shown that investors often project their outlooks too far into the future and allow that to bias their decisions. A classic example of this occurred in December 1996, when Federal Reserve Chairman Alan Greenspan made a speech to the American Enterprise Institute for Public Policy. In that speech he coined the phrase "irrational exuberance" as a warning that stock market prices were inflated compared to fundamental valuations.

Few investors listened because they were convinced that the market would climb. After a brief decline, the market continued to climb higher, thus prompting Greenspan to consider that perhaps stock prices weren't inflated after all.

In September 1998 at the Haas Annual Business Faculty Research Dialog at the University of California, Greenspan stated, *"Some of those who advocate a 'new economy' attribute it generally to technological innovations and breakthroughs in globalization that raise productivity and offer new capacity on demand and that have, accordingly, removed pricing power from the world's producers on a more lasting basis."*

The more prophetic words from Greenspan came moments later. He said, *"There is one important caveat to the notion that we live in a new economy, and that's human psychology."*[1]

People were convinced that the market would do nothing but continue to climb. And it did—until human psychology took over. From 2000 to 2002, the market shed about 35% of its value,

---

[1] *Alan Greenspan Chair of the U.S. Federal Reserve Board Speech at the University of California at Berkeley September 4, 1998*

leaving investor accounts in shambles, but from the fall of 2002 until the end of 2007, the market gained 86%.

Think of the consequences if you were under-diversified when the market was losing 35% because you firmly believed it would continue to grow in the new economy. To make matters worse, what if you sold near the bottom and were afraid to re-enter the market during the subsequent rally? These are very real (and highly likely) situations that occur when investing on emotion.

Fear of Loss Is an Emotion

Daniel Kahneman and Amos Tversky in their book *Choices, Values, and Frames* show that people strongly prefer avoiding losses to acquiring gains. In other words, people suffer from loss aversion. The pain felt from a $500 loss is far greater than the excitement from a $500 gain. Therefore, people concentrate their efforts on avoiding losses.

In Kahneman and Tversky's research, a sample of their undergraduates refused to stake $10 on the toss of a coin if they stood to win less than $30. The attractiveness of the gain was not sufficient to compensate for the aversion to the possible loss.

This behavior shouldn't be too surprising, but things got really interesting when the researchers decided to challenge people on their beliefs by adding a related question—with a twist.

They asked people if they would prefer an 85% chance of losing $1,000 (and therefore a 15% chance of losing nothing) or a guaranteed loss of $800. A large majority preferred the gamble over the sure loss.

This is risk-seeking because the expectation of the gamble is less painful than the expectation of loss. This shows a critically important point about human psychology and investing: Investors' aversion to loss is so great that it overcomes their aversion to risk. In other words, people despise taking losses so much that they'll overstep their risk boundaries in hopes of avoiding the loss.

That's perhaps the most dangerous of all combined approaches you could take to the financial markets. Unfortunately, it's how we're programmed to behave. In working with your employees, it is essential that both you and they understand this principle of human psychology.

Short of wandering aimlessly through the mountains of Tibet searching for a Buddhist monk, can people completely detach from their emotions? We all know that is impossible;

however, there are a number of methods that help take emotion out of the investment process.

The most important issue just may be the admission that we have a choice in the risk of loss. We either expose ourselves to the **risk of volatility** or to the **risk of lost opportunity** to do better than bank interest-rate returns. The investment process could be viewed as a marriage between one's psychological comfort with the journey and the financial rewards of one's intended destination.

Volatility is known to have the taste of either chocolate milk or sour milk, depending on the current temporary direction of Wall Street. The risk of volatility is very different than the risk of loss for the investor with a long-term horizon.

Chapter 3: Develop a Winning Strategy

Companies have embraced technology to automate the assembly line and implement efficiencies like just-in-time production. Likewise, financial professionals have developed programs and processes to handle aspects of investing. Computers buy and sell millions of shares of stock each day based on market "set" points. Many mutual fund companies take programmed trading to a new level and allow computer models to manage funds by trading particular stocks or indices. Losses are limited, and profits are taken based on specified parameters.

Computers are, in fact, an excellent tool for investment decisions because they follow specific instructions and do things automatically. This reduces the chances that the human emotions of fear and greed get in the way. Automating the process is simple and prudent for both the employees and the fiduciaries.

Here are some ways in which plan sponsors can help employees automate investment decisions to eliminate emotions, which will ultimately help them avoid making costly investment mistakes.

The Benefits of Automatic

Hockey players are required to skate, shoot, pass, and stick handle, all at the same time. After years of practice, they do each instinctively. If you have to think about what you are doing on the ice, it is too late, and the play is over.

Instincts play as large a role in other aspects of life as they do in hockey. The habits we form during practice sessions, good or bad, show up under the bright lights on game night. As the saying goes, "Practice does not make perfect; practice makes permanent." Many marvel at the ability of hockey players and how they move and shoot like they do. They can play like that because they practice properly until everything becomes automatic.

The design of your 401(k) plan will ultimately impact your employees' saving and investment behaviors. The following automatic features are a powerful way to have a positive influence:

1. Automatic enrollment
2. Automatic QDIA (qualified default investment alternative)
3. Automatic escalation
4. Automatic re-enrollment

We recommend that plan sponsors carefully review each of these automatic features before deciding which ones they want to implement in their plan to help employees prepare for their retirement.

Based on past experience, many employers have resisted implementing such features in their plan designs, fearing that doing so may upset their employees. However, just the opposite is the case. Not using automatic features is more detrimental to employees.

With meaningful communications, employees will appreciate that they need coaching to create the retirements they want. The absolute worse time for an employee to figure this out is when it's too late to change the outcome. It is imperative that employers create an environment where it is more meaningful for employees to save and make wise investment decisions.

You will find a resource section in the back of the book that explains the positive benefits of having automatic features in your 401(k) plan*.*

One resource is the website www.retirementmadesimpler.org. The site was created by AARP, FINRA (Financial Industry Regulatory Authority), and RSP (Retirement Security Project). They wanted to collectively use the strengths of each organization to help plan sponsors and their employees save more effectively for retirement.

They state on the website, "We know the automatic 401(k)s work. Participation rates *typically soar to between 85 – 95%* with these types of plans." The site also offers employers a 401(k) Automatic Toolkit and success stories of companies that have implemented these for their employees.

Here are the automatic features explained in greater detail.

Automatic Enrollment

The first feature is easy to understand and could improve every employer's plan.

Here is how it works:

Companies that have implemented automatic enrollment have discovered that they have increased enrollment and that about 20% of their employees choose to opt out of the plan. Those who are automatically enrolled are also far less likely to stop contributing money toward their retirements once they start. When a new employee becomes eligible to participate in the plan, they receive a letter notifying them that they will be automatically enrolled. Unless new employees notify you that they do not want to participate, each enrollment moving forward is automatic.

The prior method—asking a participant to complete an enrollment form when eligible—was inefficient and a waste of time for both the employer and the employee, and it didn't contribute to desired results. All you need to decide is the contribution level at which to set the automatic enrollment. We believe that it is prudent to enroll employees at a level at which they will maximize any company match. For example, if a company has a matching contribution level of *50%* up to *6%* of contributions, they should automatically enroll new employees at the *6%* contribution level so that each will receive the full company matching contribution.

Some employers unfortunately worry that automatically deducting money from an employee's paycheck will upset them; however, like exercise, the key is getting someone to start in the first place. The goal should always be to implement processes that assist employees in saving enough money for retirement. The first step is getting them in the plan.

Automatic QDIA

If an employee doesn't choose how their money is to be invested in the plan, they would automatically be invested in the company's qualified default investment alternative (QDIA).

The Department of Labor (DOL) defines a QDIA as an investment fund or model portfolio that is designed to provide both long-term appreciation and capital preservation through a mix of equity and fixed income exposures.

A variety of investment options may qualify as your 401(k) plan's QDIA, which may include balanced funds, lifestyle funds (conservative, moderate, growth, aggressive), and target date funds (2030, 2040, 2050, etc.).

A majority of employees simply don't have the necessary knowledge and experience to construct a well-diversified investment portfolio. Because of that, we continue to believe that one of the best long-term choices for most employees is to invest in a target date fund, which is tailored to their anticipated retirement date. The benefit of a target date fund is that it automatically adjusts its exposure from equity to fixed income as an investor approaches retirement. It is an excellent "automatic pilot" option for employees who rarely analyze or assess their progress or needs after they enroll.

Automatic Escalation

Of all of the automatic features, this is probably the most beneficial because employees need assistance to accumulate, as much as possible, an adequate amount of money for their retirements.

If an employer automatically enrolls new employees at *3%*, or even *6%* as per our previous example, it leaves a fairly sizeable gap before reaching a recommended *10%* savings rate. On the flip side—based on experience—if you tell employees that they need to increase their savings rate to *10%* immediately, they are going to think it is unrealistic. Most have expenses that have built up over time that prevent them from deferring *10%* of their pay.

I've learned that employees benefit more from the "automatic pilot" discipline of starting at a level at which they feel comfortable (*3% to 5%*) and then incrementally increasing that savings rate by *1%* a year until they reach the recommended *10%* rate.

There can be a significant difference at times between what we intend to do and what we actually get done. Employees may forget to increase their contributions a year later or put off the increase until "later." Human nature can impede their progress. That's why it's so important to automate the *1%* savings rate increase decision for them.

The Power of Auto Escalation

Assumptions : $50,000 / yr Salary | 0.0% Annual Salary Increase | 6.0% Rate of Return

AGE	CARLOS (SAVES 10% PER YEAR)			NANCY (SAVES 5% NOW + 1% / YR TO 10%)			DAN (SAVES 5% PER YEAR)		
	ANNUAL DEFERRAL	GAIN OR LOSS*	ACCOUNT BALANCE	ANNUAL DEFERRAL	GAIN OR LOSS*	ACCOUNT BALANCE	ANNUAL DEFERRAL	GAIN OR LOSS*	ACCOUNT BALANCE
30	$5,000	$150	$5,150	$2,500	$75	$2,575	$2,500	$75	$2,575
35	$5,000	$1,892	$35,923	$5,000	$1,349	$26,333	$2,500	$946	$17,961
40	$5,000	$4,223	$77,104	$5,000	$3,496	$64,270	$2,500	$2,111	$38,552
45	$5,000	$7,342	$132,214	$5,000	$6,370	$115,039	$2,500	$3,671	$66,107
50	$5,000	$11,517	$205,963	$5,000	$10,216	$182,980	$2,500	$5,758	$102,981
55	$5,000	$17,103	$304,655	$5,000	$15,362	$273,899	$2,500	$8,552	$152,328
60	$5,000	$24,579	$436,729	$5,000	$22,249	$395,570	$2,500	$12,289	$218,364
65	$5,000	$34,583	$613,472	$5,000	$31,466	$558,393	$2,500	$17,292	$306,736

RETIREMENT SAVINGS >> $613,472

RETIREMENT SAVINGS >> $558,393

RETIREMENT SAVINGS >> $306,736

* Annual gains/losses were calculated using average account balance.

The preceding chart demonstrates the power of education and inspiring your people to take advantage of proper planning and automation. The power of this incremental increase over time is remarkable.

In this example we compare the long-term results of three employees: Carlos, Nancy, and Dan. They are all 30 years old and will earn $50,000 each year until they retire at age 65. During that time let's assume they earn an average annual return of 6% in their 401(k) accounts.

During enrollment, they are reminded about the importance of saving 10% of their earnings each year. Carlos is quick to respond, "I can save 10% of my income every year. Not a problem." He starts immediately and maintains his contribution level. By the time he retires, he has $613,472 in his account.

Nancy, however, indicates that she can't "afford" 10% right now. After some thought she says, "I can only save 5% this year, and I want to increase my contributions by 1% annually for the next 5 years." After setting up her auto-pilot plan, she has $558,393 with which to retire.

Dan also starts with a 5% contribution and intends to increase it by 1% annually; however, he doesn't follow through and remains at that level for the next 35 years. As Dan reaches retirement, the "seeds" he planted in his 401(k) account bring a "crop" of $306,736.

Human nature has made Dan's 401(k) account $251,657 LESS than Nancy's automatic-pilot account at retirement. It's clear that Dan's retirement account results cost him more than the incremental automatic increases would have cost his lifestyle while he was working.

This is why automatic escalation is so important. When employees see the side-by-side comparison, the impact is motivating. They quickly realize that they don't want to make Dan's mistake and many immediately sign up for automatic escalation.

It's important to remember that an employee **can opt out of automatic escalation at any time**. The participants **always** have the ability to make changes. As with any of the automatic features mentioned, an employee simply needs to notify the plan sponsor that they would like to change one or more automatic features.

Automatic Re-Enrollment

Again, it's important to understand that a majority of employees in a 401(k) plan do not have the knowledge or experience to make prudent investment choices regarding retirement. They don't have the necessary information, nor do they take the time to understand when to adjust their asset allocations over extended periods of time when their "time horizon" and "risk tolerance" change during their careers.

A multitude of factors go into making sound investment decisions. In order to be effective, employees would need to understand how to build well-diversified portfolios, how to manage investment fees and expenses, when to re-balance their portfolios, how to analyze and manage risk, and what that means in terms of adjusting asset allocations over a long period of time. Those employees who lack the proper understanding of investing would be far better served if they had just invested their money in target-date funds.

Re-enrollment is a feature designed to assist those less-experienced investors. Once a year the company sends out a notification to participants, informing them that they will have an open enrollment period. If an employee doesn't respond and inform the plan sponsor not to change their current investment allocation, then **100%** of their money in their 401(k) account is automatically transferred into the QDIA—in this case, the target-date fund based on their expected retirement.

Studies show that when automatic re-enrollment is implemented, about **_70% to 80%_** of employees will not opt out and will let their assets be transferred into target-date funds. This is good for a couple of reasons: The employee benefits in the long-term, and plan fiduciaries receive protection for implementing automatic features.

For employers who are concerned about this feature because it moves employees out of funds they originally selected, please remember that you will receive fiduciary protection under the Pension Protection Act of 2006, provided (a) you give the appropriate notice, (b) employees have the ability to opt out, (c) the target-date funds are set in the plan as QDIA, and (d) the plan sponsor is performing ongoing prudent due diligence reviews of the investment options and documenting their process.

Careful Consideration

Automating aspects of 401(k) investing provides a huge benefit to the majority of employees and the company itself. As with anything, there are pros and cons, and it's important to consider any potential drawbacks.

One of the biggest drawbacks to any automated process is that it tends to disconnect employees from setting goals and making important decisions along the way. Automatic 401(k) features cannot replace the need for employees to maintain active roles. They still need to determine their retirement aspirations, their levels of contribution to get there, and the levels of volatility they wish to accept.

These processes won't automatically bring success to employees, but they'll certainly make some of the most important decisions easier and more consistent. Above all, they'll have the opportunity to reduce the emotional mistakes that individual investors make and limit the negative impacts they can have on an employee's retirement.

The Magic of the Stretch Match

This feature really gets to the core of behavioral finance and human psychology because there is an "incentive" for employees to deduct a higher percentage of their pay. By adjusting their current company matching formula, a plan sponsor can begin to directly influence the rate at which employees save.

If the goal is to help employees have proud retirements, an employer can influence behavior by increasing the current company match to leverage higher employee savings levels. For instance, if a company is currently matching *50%* on every dollar up to the first *6%* of an employee's contribution, the company isn't creating any incentive for employees to save more than **6%** of their pay.

Employers who offer a company match can assess whether modifications to their matching formulas could create a positive influence on the savings behavior of employees. The following chart illustrates how the stretch match works.

Stretch Match Design

DEFERRAL RATE	CURRENT COMPANY MATCH	STRETCH COMPANY MATCH
10%	–	25%
9%	–	25%
8%	–	25%
7%	–	25%
6%	50%	25%
5%	50%	25%
4%	50%	25%
3%	50%	25%
2%	50%	50%
1%	50%	50%
	MATCH 50% ON FIRST 6%	50% ON FIRST 2% 25% ON NEXT 8%

When the employer matches **50%** of the first **6%** of an employee contribution, the maximum employer cost is **3%** of the participant salary. If the employer adjusts the matching contributions to *50%* of the first *2%* and *25%* of the next *8%* of pay, the employee has an incentive to increase their contribution, which helps them enhance their retirement funding. Ultimately, the out-of-pocket costs for the company will not exceed *3%* of participant salary.

Understand that some employees may not appreciate revisions to the company match. Some may view it as 'forcing' them to save more than they feel comfortable with. It is also important to communicate to them that an employee who is saving *6%* of their income with their company match of *50%* is actually receiving *9%*. Communication can assist your employees in realizing that you are enhancing their retirement potential, not detracting from it.

It is also recommended to ask your third-party administrator (TPA) to find out whether you are currently electing to contribute Safe Harbor minimum contributions to your 401(k) plan. By switching your matching formula to a "stretch match," you will most likely be surrendering your Safe Harbor, and the plan would be subject to Actual Deferral Percentage (ADP) and/or Actual Contribution Percentage (ACP) testing.

Winning Retirement Plan Process

Your company-sponsored retirement plan can be tricky business without a detailed process. A successful retirement plan will reinforce your commitment to employees and will help you attract and retain the best talent.

When you enlist our services, you gain a valuable ally and a time-saving resource, who will help you develop and maintain a solid strategy for your retirement plan.

[KEY 1] PLAN EVALUATION
- Plan review and needs assessment
- Review current provider
- Report initial findings

[KEY 2] IMPLEMENTATION
- Prepare an Investment Policy Statement (if necessary)
- Select investment options
- Manage plan sponsor expectations

[KEY 3] ONGOING SERVICE
- Quarterly fund performance evaluations
- Quarterly plan sponsor meetings and annual plan review
- Unbiased investment advice regarding your fund lineup
- Monitoring provider enhancements
- Monitoring industry trends

- Plan sponsor service support/problem resolution
- Employee pre-retirement planning

As a fiduciary, it is important for a plan sponsor to manage risk by implementing and following a process.

Establishing an Investment Policy Statement

ERISA doesn't specifically require plan sponsors to have an Investment Policy Statement for their retirement plans, but establishing one and following it goes a long way in demonstrating that a plan sponsor has implemented a prudent process by which investment decisions are made.

Chapter 4: Properly Position Members of the Team

The Vision

During my coaching years, I developed a process that created a winning team culture. A culture is the expression of a team's values, attitudes, and beliefs about sports and competition. The culture determines the focus, grounded in a recognized sense of mission and shared goals. For example, the team could have a goal of qualifying for regionals or winning the championship. Defining this culture provides the team with a superior mental focus needed to have an edge that other teams don't have. This will help them win more games. Creating a focused winning culture is a good habit to practice in sports, in business, and in life.

If you apply the same principles to your 401(k) plan, it will position your employees to obtain positive habits of saving for retirement. In this scenario, everyone is a winner.

Members of the Team

While I coached the Arrowhead High School boys' varsity hockey team in 2008-09, we faced many challenges during the season. We overcame most of them through repetition, repetition, repetition. Undoubtedly, we had great team chemistry that year, and it didn't hurt that our goalie was one of the best in the state. We also had a very dangerous offensive line, extremely disciplined players on defense, and took very few penalties. Like most teams, one of the biggest issues we faced was that everyone wanted to score goals. That's understandable, but we reminded our team constantly that defense wins championships and instilled the work ethic and conditioning necessary to protect our net.

After countless meetings with players to discuss their individual roles, we ultimately positioned everyone where they gave us the best chance for success. The results were almost immediate. We outscored opponents 22 to 2 in the last 4 games to complete the regular season at 15-5-0 and began steamrolling through the regional and sectional playoff games on our way to the state championship in Madison.

Success with any team is based upon its players and their ability to work together. As much as any coach would love for this to happen automatically, it takes a lot of work to guide individuals at various levels with divergent personalities and skill sets—all operating as a cohesive unit. In coaching I learned the foundations that helped me generate greater teamwork among my players.

I learned that clearly defining individual roles and personal growth plans worked particularly well when developing a team. Each position on the team has a specific role and responsibility that will enhance or detract from the team during a game. When a player understands that expectations exist for them to rise to the next skill level, they are more apt to meet the challenge, therefore becoming a better team player.

Here are the role players for your 401(k) plan:

Understanding the Roles of 401(k) Service Providers

401(k) plans are complex and often difficult to understand due to the number of service providers and regulations required to make a plan run and keep it in compliance, not to mention the long list of industry acronyms that get thrown into 401(k) discussions and documents. We're often asked by plan sponsors to clarify who all of the service providers are on their plan, what they do, and how they are paid.

Record Keeper (Plan Provider)

The record keeper is sometimes referred to as your primary 401(k) provider, as they are typically the most visible provider on your plan. Their role is to manage and track the data within the 401(k) plan and communicate that data with the other necessary parties. The website where employees log into and where payroll data is uploaded is almost always managed by your record keeper.

Record keepers are usually paid by a direct annual base fee and per-participant fees, but can also have asset-based fees that are either paid from participant balances or indirectly from the mutual funds in the plan. Typically, you can elect whether recordkeeping fees are paid by the employer or the employees. Some record keepers are also TPA firms. This is so the data and compliance work is all done under the same roof.

Third-Party Administrator (TPA)

The TPA or third-party administrator manages most of the plan compliance. As mentioned, some TPA firms are record keepers as well. Compliance work consists of things like preparing your annual 401(k) tax filing (your 5500), managing plan documents, and performing required annual non-discrimination testing on the plan. In many cases, your TPA firm is a local company separate from your record keeper.

While they typically bill the company directly, TPA fees can also be paid by plan participants.

Their fees usually involve an annual base fee, a per-participant fee. We've also seen TPAs charge asset-based fees on occasion; these are usually paid directly from participant accounts.

Custodian

The custodian on a 401(k) plan is like a bank. They are responsible for moving the money. They move funds from the company's bank account into the individual investment accounts, as they receive instructions from the record keeper, based on what the participants and sponsor have elected. You don't usually have significant interaction with this service provider, other than opening a custodial account and giving them permission to transfer (ACH) funds from your company account. They are typically paid a small, asset-based fee, which is deducted from participant accounts.

Financial Advisor/Broker

The financial advisor on your plan is the registered and licensed professional who has the responsibility to provide investment advice to plan sponsors and some give advice to employees. Not all 401(k) plans have a financial advisor, although many do. They can be a great resource for employees and your internal investment committee. In many cases, they are also the person who sold the plan to the company.

Most financial advisors receive an asset-based fee that is paid directly from participant accounts (better) or indirectly from the mutual funds in the plan (worse). Any time a service provider is paid based on the funds they are selling it represents a conflict of interest and shouldn't be allowed in a 401(k) plan. Unfortunately, indirect compensation is the norm for many 401(k) plans.

Auditor

Not all plans have or need a 401(k) auditor. You are only required to perform an annual audit on your 401(k) plan if you have over 100 eligible participants. If you do require an audit, the auditor is typically a local accounting firm that has experience in this space. You are also not required to use the same auditor each year, though it can often save you costs and create efficiencies when you work with the same firm.

Audit costs are typically billed directly to the plan sponsor, though they can also be paid by participants or forfeitures if there are enough to effectively cover the cost.

ERISA Attorney

Not all companies use an ERISA attorney on their 401(k) plans. In many cases, they simply trust that their TPA and record keeper have a capable attorney that is reviewing and monitoring plan documents and procedures. Unfortunately, if those parties don't have a capable attorney and you adopt a plan document that has issues, it's usually you (the plan sponsor) who is legally responsible for the consequences.

Before proceeding without an ERISA attorney, you should ask your providers if documents have been reviewed and approved by an ERISA attorney. In many cases, they can even show you an IRS determination letter, certifying the veracity and compliant nature of the document. Should you decide to use an outside ERISA attorney for a plan or document review, they typically bill hourly, and the good ones have a healthy billing rate.

Fiduciary

An entire book could be written about different plan fiduciaries and their roles. In general, a 401(k) plan fiduciary is someone that has legal responsibility to act in the sole interest of your employees. One of their primary jobs is to select, monitor, and benchmark the service providers on the plan. Despite what you may think, in most cases, the service providers mentioned above and below are not actually plan fiduciaries; they are merely service providers. While they do significant work on the plan, they are rarely held responsible when it comes to 401(k) lawsuits or audits by government entities. In most 401(k) plans, the plan sponsor carries all of the administrative and investment fiduciary roles and has exposure to the risk and work associated with those roles.

Plan Consultant/Benefits Broker

In some cases, plans will hire or include an independent consultant who helps with various plan duties. Sometimes benefits brokers act in this role. Their duties can include enrollment meetings, employee education, plan benchmarking, and various other functions.

Usually these consultants are paid a flat fee or an asset-based fee that can be paid by the plan sponsor or participants. If there is a consultant being paid on your plan who isn't providing any services, you should look into it. Anyone receiving an ongoing fee in your 401(k) plan should be providing an ongoing service.

As a plan sponsor and fiduciary, managing all of the parties on your 401(k) plan can be complex and difficult at times. Hopefully now you have a better understanding of who they are and what they do.

Plan Sponsors

In sports, it's simple for even the most uninformed person to understand who has a winning team because the score is published on a large screen in bright lights for everyone to see. It is not as easy to put a total team together until you have an understanding of all of the components involved. As a coach, I counted on my assistant coaches and team players for support and communication.

I find that plan sponsors want and need guidance, as well as support. Here are some areas which plan sponsors look to advisors for communication:

- Sponsors want to understand their role in the plan…so we explain the need for sound decision-making and a prudent process.

- Sponsors want a clear, objective way to maintain their lineup…so we monitor your process and explain the pros and cons of having an Investment Policy Statement, the need to follow it, and your options as a plan fiduciary.

- Sponsors want a clear understanding of who is and who is not a fiduciary on their plan...so we don't mince words. For starters, it's you and anyone on the plan committee. You can't dodge this responsibility, but you can manage the risk by implementing and following a structured strategy. We provide the guidance every step of the way.

- Sponsors want expert help designing and following an impactful plan document...so we partner with the industry's leading third-party administrators, record keepers, ERISA attorneys, and certified public accountants to get you the right answers at the right time.

Chapter 5: Execute the Game Plan Consistently

The Preparation

Throughout the playoffs, we prepared for each game in the same ways: We watched video on the opponent to identify their systems and tendencies, we reviewed our strategy and game plan, and we had a team meal the night before. Because of all of the preparation, each member of the team knew their role and entered the state tournament with extreme confidence.

The team won the first two games (4-0 and 6-2) and was now in the championship game. Players were ready, and the execution of the game plan was nearly flawless as they rolled in the championship game by a score of 5-1. One individual on the team even broke a pair of state tournament scoring records (Most Goals and Most Points) that had stood since 1971.

When offering a retirement plan, it is important to be consistent. This can be most challenging for an employer to meet their responsibilities as a plan sponsor. Understanding of the basic rules of the game, specifically the Employee Retirement Income Security Act (ERISA), will help those who manage an employee benefit plan.

The Essential Elements of a Plan

- Have a written plan that describes the structure of the benefit.
  - Include guidelines for the day-to-day operations of the plan.
- Arrange a trust for the plan's assets.
- Develop a recordkeeping system.
- Keep up-to-date on the changing DOL regulations and the IRS Codes.
- Monitor investments on a consistent basis.
- Know who is and who is not a fiduciary.
- Document, document, document.

Now that the basic fundamentals have been established, it is time to focus on how to best apply those principles.

Best Practices

First, the plan sponsor and advisor should have and follow a sound Investment Policy Statement, rigorously monitor investments, and document all decision-making processes. This document serves as the foundation for the entire operation of the plan. Take minutes when meeting with your advisor or reviewing your plan. During group education sessions, take attendance, and keep an organized folder with 401(k) documentation. Be familiar with your plan document, whether it is drawn up in-house or by a service provider. Periodically reviewing the document will ensure that it remains current.

A plan's assets must be held in trust to ensure that the assets are used solely to benefit the participants. The trust must have at least one trustee to handle contributions, plan investments, and distributions. Since the financial integrity of the plan depends on the trustee, selecting a trustee is one of the most important decisions you will make in establishing a plan.

An accurate recordkeeping system will track and properly attribute contributions, earnings and losses, plan investments, expenses, and benefit distributions. If a contract administrator or financial institution assists in managing the plan, that entity typically will keep the required records.

You must notify employees who are eligible to participate in the plan about certain benefits, rights, and features. A summary plan description must be provided to all participants. This summary will inform participants about the plan and how it operates. Typically, this summary is created with the plan document.

Thousands of audits are conducted every year by the Internal Revenue Service (IRS) and the Department of Labor (DOL), focusing on employee benefit retirement plans. The IRS audit's focal point is on compliance with the Internal Revenue Code. In DOL audits the focal point is on violations of the Employee Retirement Income Security Act of 1974, as amended (ERISA). In past years, both agencies have increasingly been focused on the monitoring controls that employers maintain for their employee benefit plans.

Specifically, the IRS is increasing its focus on ensuring that retirement plan sponsors maintain monitoring controls to ensure their plans comply with the Code. Agents look for documented practices and procedures that prevent errors or that quickly flag errors before they result in large financial consequences. Agents want to see evidence of actual checks and balances, specific and tangible monitoring controls, and retention of records or proof that internal controls have been implemented.

Even more than the IRS, the DOL is concerned with proper process and procedures. In some cases, the end result may not seem as important as the procedures that the plan sponsor followed on the way. Like the IRS, the DOL looks for documented practices and procedures that prevent errors or that quickly flag errors before they result in large financial consequences.

The plan sponsor is ultimately responsible for ensuring that its retirement plan complies with the law in both form and operation. Plan sponsors should establish and follow a process for reviewing their investment lineup at reasonable intervals.

How Plan Sponsors Put Themselves at Risk

In hockey you are taught to play "with your head on a swivel." Not doing so is a surefire way to cost your team the game or put yourself at risk of serious injury. In 1989 I was playing in an exhibition preseason game with the Vancouver Canucks at the Bradley Center against the Los Angeles Kings.

At the time, Wayne Gretzky (The Great One) was on the Kings. In the second period I was supposed to be covering him. I got caught 'puck watching' and lost track of him for a split second. That was all it took. He got behind me, received a bullet pass, and screamed toward our net. To prevent the breakaway, I quickly slashed his stick and pulled him to the ice.

After I had served my penalty, I heard a gruff voice from behind me yell that if I did that again, they would be carrying me out on a stretcher! As I jerked my head around, there stood Gretzky's enforcer, Marty McSorley. Not only did I put my team at risk by puck watching and taking a penalty, I put my own well-being at risk. Lesson learned; nobody wanted the wrath of Marty McSorley!

At a recent meeting, a company executive stated, "Our 401(k) retirement plan is 'back-burner business,' and I do not have time to spend on it, as I have more important things like my P&L to worry about."

I absolutely agree. That company executive is responsible for the performance of the company and spends most of his energy focused on growing and developing the business. There is a never-ending flood of more pressing issues demanding his immediate attention, but this perpetuates the ignore-it-until-it-becomes-a-problem approach with regards to their 401(k) plan. "Important" and "urgent" issues are juggled daily by all of us. 401(k) plans can be similar to one's car, which needs specific maintenance to prevent a major breakdown at a very inconvenient time.

Most plan sponsors are well aware of their fiduciary responsibilities, along with the horror stories out there about personal liability. They may or may not know that litigation of plan fiduciaries is growing like a wild fire.
Eleven major class-action lawsuits were filed in federal courts around the country against 401(k) sponsors in the fourth quarter of 2015 alone*.

All involved alleged fiduciary breaches of, among other things, excessive fees benefitting service providers in violation of the Employee Retirement Income and Security Act of 1974 (ERISA).

Employees Winning 401(k) Lawsuits Over High Fees and Other Shortcomings
www.mainstreet.com/article/employees-winning-401k-more-lawsuits-over-high-fees-and-other-shortcomings

While this may look like exposure for plan sponsors and ERISA fiduciaries, it is important to keep in mind that these cases are much more difficult for plaintiffs to win if prudent fiduciary practices are in place and implemented.

How You Can Help Protect Yourself

Responsible plan fiduciaries benefit by understanding their fiduciary obligations that are imposed in law and regulation. Although not specifically required under ERISA, we recommend that plan sponsors hire an advisor to assist them in monitoring the investment lineup. For additional coverage, this advisor/coach should sign on as co-fiduciary, provide written plan reviews on a regular basis, and put all recommendations in writing. In addition, the plan sponsor and advisor should have and follow a sound Investment Policy Statement, rigorously monitor investments, and document all decision-making processes.

ERISA does not judge investment performance in hindsight, so some of the arguments over imprudent investment selection are easy to disprove by following a sound process.

The cases that have won generally involve egregious fiduciary breaches, such as using retail classes of funds for plans that could easily have chosen directly comparable institutional shares. Disproportionately over-charging participants for certain funds in the investment lineup is clearly imprudent.

Defense Can Help You Win

In sports it's understood that defense wins championships. Nowhere is that more true than in hockey. Based on my experience playing the game and coaching, the goalie is absolutely the most important player on the ice. His mission is to stop everything directed at him in order to protect the team's net. Jacques Plante, a famous goaltender who played for the Montreal Canadians from 1953-63, summed up how truly difficult the job is with the following quote:
"How would you like it if, at your job, every time you made the slightest mistake a little red light went on over your head and 18,000 people stood up and screamed at you?"

What many don't realize is that Plante was considered to be one of the most important innovators in hockey. He was the first NHL goaltender to wear a goaltender mask on a regular basis and developed and tested many versions of the mask with the assistance of other experts. He was also the first NHL goaltender to regularly play the puck outside his crease in support of his team's defensemen and often instructed his teammates from behind the play.

The defense's goal to protect the net should also be the focus of a company-sponsored 401(k) retirement plan. Unfortunately, many have neglected to identify current potential exposures.

Our hands-on process helps plan sponsors and investment committees identify what they are doing well and what aspects of their plans need additional structure and focus. As a 3(21) co-fiduciary, we are also in a position to take the heavy burden and share the responsibility of monitoring the investment performance of your plan. By having this done consistently and delivered on a quarterly basis, along with any fund replacement recommendations, you demonstrate that prudent care was taken in selecting investment options for participants.

Organizing Your Retirement Plan Fiduciary File

As a plan sponsor and fiduciary of your company's retirement plan, keeping an up-to-date fiduciary file is critical. One of the first things the DOL wants to know is if you have a prudent process and if you follow it on a consistent basis.

While this list below is by no means exhaustive, employers who use this checklist and have these documents organized will enjoy a level of peace of mind about their compliance with applicable law.

1. DOCUMENTS
   - Plan document
   - IRS Determination Letter
   - Summary plan description
   - IRS Forms 5500 (last 3 taxable years)
   - Investment Policy Statement
   - 404(c) Policy Statement and Notice
   - Service provider contracts
   - Nondiscrimination Test results
   - Summary annual report
   - Plan assets

2. ADMINISTRATIVE
- Evidence of employer contributions
- Distribution documents
- Audit results
- Participant complaints
- Fiduciary liability insurance contract
- Correspondence

3. PARTICIPANT COMMUNICATION
- Enrollment material
- Documentation of communication events
- Attendance at educational meetings

4. INVESTMENT OPTIONS
- Current fund lineup
- Fund performance reports and plan reviews
- Investment committee meeting minutes
- Plan Expenses — 408(b)(2)

The Benefits of a Winning Game Plan

A winning game plan facilitates participants to retire on time, with enough resources to do so. Employees who are able to retire on time allow remaining employees to advance, which reduces frustration for all. Happy employees are more productive. This reduces the costs to the company of hiring and training new employees.

If you are an owner of a company, the CFO, or head of human resources, your time and energy are best spent on successfully running your company and not being tied up in the retirement plan. Under ERISA Sections 402(c) (3), a named fiduciary may formally delegate certain responsibilities to a prudent, expert service provider. This is an excellent way to outsource responsibility for managing the often time-consuming process of monitoring investments offered in the plan. These fiduciary service providers can be:

1. A 3(21) non-discretionary fiduciary

2. A 3(38) full discretionary fiduciary

3. A 3(16) plan administrator

As a registered investment advisor, we take on **3(21)** limited scope fiduciary responsibilities in regard to the investment options offered in the plan. Our services are spelled out in greater detail in our service agreement. We manage the entire due diligence process as part of our extensive service model, so plan sponsors can focus on other elements of their strategic operating plan.

Chapter 6: Monitor Results and Document

Monitoring Effectively Includes:

- Communicating frequently with the plan's service provider to ensure that all relevant data is provided timely and accurately
- Reviewing the plan document annually to ensure the plan is operating according to its terms
- Making the service provider and other relevant parties aware of any changes to the plan in a timely manner
- Developing a communication mechanism for exchanging information with the service provider

Documenting Effectively Includes:

Monitoring results is not simply printing a report to evaluate the funds. The quarterly report you receive consists of a multitude of data that will help monitor the overall plan objectives.

The term "process" is used repeatedly throughout much of the ERISA reading. IRS agents will look for documented practices. The DOL asks for an Investment Policy Statement, which simply means a written process. In its audits it is clear that the focus is on the prudence of process to ensure sponsors maintain internal controls. In Donovan v. Cunningham, the 5th Circuit Court opined, "[ERISA's] test of prudence...is one of conduct." While this case and the quoted Interpretive Bulletin focus on the prudence of the investments, the Court discusses the process, not the result. It should be further considered that the courts consider facts and circumstances when evaluating prudence. It would be difficult to argue a prudent process for a service if you did not have a mechanism to track whether the services and associated activities were performed as outlined.

Plan sponsors have to create a discernable process that includes reviewing your investment lineup on a regular basis and making prudent investment decisions for participants based on detailed quarterly fund evaluations.

To assist with monitoring results, you can hire someone to manage the plan. If you hire the right advisor, you share the fiduciary responsibility. You should document your selection process and monitor the services provided.

Items to Consider When Selecting an Advisor:

- Information about the firm itself: affiliations, financial condition, experience with 401(k) plans, and assets under administration
- A description of business practices: how plan assets will be invested if the firm will manage plan investments or how participant investment directions will be handled
- Information about the quality of prospective providers: the identity, experience, and qualifications of the professionals who will be handling the plan's account; any recent litigation or enforcement action that has been taken against the firm; the firm's experience or performance record; if the firm plans to work with any of its affiliates in handling the plan's account; and whether the firm has fiduciary liability insurance.

Once hired, these are additional actions to take when monitoring a service provider:

- Evaluate any notices received from the service provider about possible changes to their compensation and the other information they provided when hired.
- Review the service provider's performance.

- Read any reports they provide.
- Check actual fees charged.
- Ask about policies and practices.
- Follow up on participant complaints.

Plan sponsors who use registered investment advisors (RIAs) indicate that they are pleased with their services and find it easy to work with them. **90%** give RIAs top marks for their knowledge of potential plan investment options and for their assistance in meeting fiduciary requirements. Despite a deep bench of services and support, RIAs are used by only ***28%*** of plan sponsors. RIAs offer an open-architecture investment platform, which is why they are ***64%*** more likely to offer investment advice to plan sponsors. In addition, they are ***60%*** more likely to advise on plan selection and design.

Our goal is to partner with plan sponsors to create a prudent process. We begin by reviewing your investment lineup and then provide an evaluation. We regularly assist you in making prudent investment decisions for participants. We prepare a detailed quarterly fund evaluation, deliver the findings, and provide unbiased investment advice in writing, so you can focus on running your business.

Whether you monitor your 401(k) plan or hire an advisor, you must have a process in place. Adopting an Investment Policy Statement (that describes criteria for the review of the fund performance and what to do if a fund is underperforming) can reduce your exposure. It is critical that the decision-making process is reflected in the investment policy statement and is followed. Document, document, document!

To Review – Here's a Summary

In our experience, we find that many companies do not have prudent processes for many reasons. Whether it is due to a lack of expertise or time, it opens the door to many questions regarding the plan. Even though the possibility of litigation may be a distant concern, it still may cross your mind.

The Strategic Game Plan – Our 5-Step Process

1. Identify current challenges and exposures.

2. Develop a winning strategy.

3. Properly position members of the team.

4. Execute the game plan consistently.

5. Monitor results and document.

We manage the entire due diligence process as part of our extensive service model, so plan sponsors can focus on their companies.

This is a Menu of what our Clients Receive:

- A partner that assumes 3(21) co-fiduciary responsibility and guides you in the ongoing process of developing and maintaining a solid strategy for your retirement plan.
- You receive an Investment Policy Statement (IPS) and a proven process for rating and monitoring the funds in the plan.
- Denali Wealth grades the investments, provides a comprehensive quarterly plan review, and meets on a regular basis to discuss the investments.
- Denali provides a written summary and recommendations each quarter.
- Denali conducts a full plan review each year and provides benchmarking information, so the client can document that we reviewed fees and determined that fees are reasonable.
- You can focus your time on growing your business.
- Helping your participants retire on time, with enough resources, assists you in attracting and retaining talented employees.

Our Clients find that working with us Results in:

- ➢ Increased contributions

- ➢ Increased participation

- ➢ Increased readiness

- ➢ Increased 401(k) compliance

Conclusion

Imagine for a second that you know little to nothing about a particular sport, and you walk past a scoreboard. Instantly, you can tell which team is ahead and which one is behind. In business and in life, just knowing the score doesn't provide all of the information needed to accurately predict the final conclusion.

We often believe that we know how to arrive where we want to go. At times, the itinerary changes without our knowledge, and we have to stop in order to get back on course. In short, we don't know what we don't know! It's often prudent to get a professional second opinion or a fresh perspective on those aspects in life about which we are *not* experts.

With the 401(k) environment ever-changing—DOL regulations; getting employees to save, so they can retire on time; and increased litigation against plan sponsors—wouldn't it be reassuring to confirm that your 401(k) plan is what you want it to be?

Many plan sponsors have long-term relationships with their advisors and believe that everything is properly in place. Having an objective review of your plan can be evidence that you are carrying out your duties prudently. In many cases, our wellness check discloses both confirmations of what aspects are fine as is and what aspects need intervention to get ahead **before** the game ends. Despite long-term relationships and/or other reasons, plan sponsors have decided to partner with us.

With growing litigation in the 401(k) arena, it is imperative that you are able to answer "***Yes***" to each of these questions. If you are unable to, then you can benefit from a second opinion.

1. **Have you examined your plan fees to ensure they are reasonable?**

2. **Do you have a Qualified Default Investment Alternative (QDIA) designated in your plan?**

3. **Do you have an evaluation process to help ensure that the offered investments meet their benchmarks as described in the Investment Policy Statement?**

4. **Does your current broker or advisor:**
    a. **Acknowledge in writing that they are a plan fiduciary?**
    b. **Provide a prudent fiduciary process for monitoring investment options?**
    c. **Provide you with investment advice and put it in writing?**

Do You Have the Right Coach?

As the level of skill and competition increase in sports, the smaller the difference becomes between a championship and second place. It usually comes down to a matter of focused execution when it really matters. That performance usually results from a process, which includes preparation for that moment and a detailed game plan that allows for that winning execution to happen.

No one can get to the championship level without the synchronized involvement of others who have also bought into and committed to the process within a culture of excellence.

The experience of the right coach can significantly elevate the potential of a group of skilled individuals to realize the dreams of the owner of the team.

Contact us today for a complementary wellness check and a second opinion on your current game plan.

Denali Wealth Management, Inc.
414-978-0020
www.denaliwm.com

Client Testimonials

"Carl and the Denali team's consultation provides our company invaluable insight and confidence that our 401(k) plan is contemporary, compliant, and within the market."

– Geoff O'Connor, CFO of Lesaffre Yeast Corp.

_____

"Carl and the team at Denali not only provide the requisite compliance, fiduciary, and investment advice for our company, OnCourse Learning, and our 401(k) participants, they provide it with a rigor, clarity, and level of delightful service that ensures the i's are dotted, the t's are crossed, and our team members are getting the right investment options and the right advice at the right time. Carl and his team do the right things right."

– Patrick Sheahan, President and CEO of OnCourse Learning

_____

"Today's employers realize financial issues are a top stress factor for their employees, affecting their physical and emotional wellbeing and thus also impacting their ability to engage in and deliver on their job responsibilities. Employers also realize that they must do more than just offer a 401(k) plan to be seen as an employer of choice. At Interior Systems Inc., we seek partners who offer broad knowledge of investment oversight and effective governance as an important element of sound risk management. Denali Wealth Management provides us with this essential plan oversight function. Their holistic approach to managing our portfolio risk and investments allows for greater transparency to our associates with better investment and fiduciary processes. This fiduciary oversight and expertise will ultimately lead to reduced operational and administrative costs and the opportunity to reinvest them in the organization's talent to advance its productivity, engagement, retention, and other employer-of-choice objectives."

– Jim Carlson, Director of Human Resources of
  Interior Systems Inc.

"Investing in a 401(k) program can be complex, overwhelming, and intimidating for employees. Carl and Denali Wealth Management understand how to keep things simple for our participants, while at the same time providing outstanding service to DELZER by focusing on the things that matter: strategy, compliance, and performance."

– Michael Delzer, President of
  Delzer Lithograph Company

"As a small business, we have too much on our plate to worry about administering our 401(k) plans. Working with Carl and his team at Denali Wealth Management has taken the administration worries away from me. With quarterly meetings to review their expertly crafted reports, we are able to stay on top of the plan performance and be assured that we are in complete compliance with the constantly changing rules and regulations."

*– David Mitchell, President and CEO of
  Monarch Machining & Production Tool*

About the Author

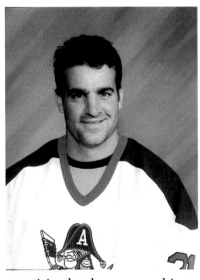

Carl Valimont is Co-Founder and President of Denali Wealth Management in Milwaukee, WI. He has over 20 years of experience in the investment management, securities brokerage, and insurance fields. Prior to forming Denali Wealth Management, he served with two other firms in the Milwaukee area, including a Financial Consultant role with RBC Wealth Management.

Carl earned his BA in business administration with a minor in marketing from the University of Massachusetts Lowell. He has passed examinations for the Series 7, 63, 65 Securities Licenses, as well as the insurance examinations. He has been named a "FIVE STAR: Best in Client Satisfaction Wealth Manager" by *Milwaukee Magazine* twice.

Carl played professional hockey for 11 years following his 4-year career at the University of Massachusetts Lowell. Carl was drafted by the

Vancouver Canucks in the 1985 NHL entry draft and played for the Milwaukee Admirals for six years before concluding his career in the Deutch Eis Hockey League in Germany. Carl coached youth hockey for 16 years in the Milwaukee area and was the head varsity hockey coach for the Arrowhead Warhawks from 1999 to 2010. He led them to a runner-up finish in 2005 and a state championship in 2009. More recently, Carl coached Milwaukee Junior Admirals U15, U16, and U18 and is currently head varsity coach at Arrowhead High School.

Carl serves on the board of the Howard G. Mullett Ice Center in Hartland, WI. He also served on the board of Tripoli Country Club and is a past president.

Resources

The U.S. Department of Labor's Employee Benefits Security Administration (EBSA) offers more information on its website and through its publications. The following are available on EBSA's website at www.dol.gov/ebsa or by calling 866-444-3272.

(1) Kruger, Justin; David Dunning: "Unskilled and Unaware of It: How Difficulties in Recognizing One's Own Incompetence Lead to Inflated Self-Assessments." *Journal of Personality and Social Psychology* (1999 Dec) v77 (6): p1121–34

psycnet.apa.org/journals/psp/77/6

Empower Institute: Lifetime Income Score VI – The Road Best Traveled
April 2016
www.empower-institute.org/research.html

***Plan Sponsor Magazine*: "Auto Enrollment Boosts Participation, Hurts Contribution Rates"**
May 2011
www.plansponsor.com/Auto_Enrollment_Boosts_Participation_Hurts_Contribution_Rates.aspx

Deloitte: Annual 401(k) Benchmarking Survey

www2.deloitte.com/us/en/pages/human-capital/articles/annual-defined-contribution-benchmarking-survey.html

U.S. Department of Labor: Sample Automatic Enrollment and Default Investment Notice

www.irs.gov/pub/irs-tege/sample_notice.pdf

U.S. Department of Labor: Meeting Your Fiduciary Responsibilities

September 2006

www.dol.gov/ebsa/pdf/fiduciaryresponsibility.pdf

U.S. Department of Labor: Default Investment Alternatives Under Participant Directed Individual Account Plans, Final Rule.

Federal Register. 29 CFR, Part 2550

October 24, 2007

www.dol.gov/ebsa/regs/fedreg/final/07-5147.pdf

401(k) Learning

http://apps.finra.org/investor_information/smart/401k/000100.asp

Made in the USA
Columbia, SC
11 May 2020